W9-AMN-795

I

D

12,930

J
817.54   Wiesner, William
W
         How silly can you be? A book of jokes. Compiled and illus.
     by William Wiesner.      Seabury ©1974
         64p    illus


         Common everyday events are spoofed in this collection of
     jokes, silly stories, and sight gags.



     1 Wit and humor    I Title

                                                        817.54

     Metro Catalog Cards

                    EAU CLAIRE DISTRICT LIBRARY

A BOOK
OF
JOKES

For Ada and Heinz

Other Seabury Books by William Wiesner

*Moon Stories*

*Turnabout*

*Hansel and Gretel: a Shadow Puppet Picture Book*

# How Silly Can You be?

## A Book of Jokes

Compiled and Illustrated
*by* WILLIAM WIESNER

*A Clarion Book*
THE SEABURY PRESS
New York

#6.95

3/16/79

Amer. Publ.

EAU CLAIRE DISTRICT LIBRARY

12,930

81345

*Second Printing*

Copyright © 1974 by William Wiesner

Printed in the United States of America

All rights reserved. No part of this book may be reproduced in any form, except for brief extracts in reviews, without the written permission of the publisher, The Seabury Press, 815 Second Avenue, New York, N. Y. 10017.

Library of Congress Cataloging in Publication Data

Wiesner, William, comp.
  How silly can you be?

    SUMMARY: Common everyday events are spoofed in this collection of jokes, silly stories, and sight gags.
    1. Wit and humor, Juvenile.   [1. Joke books]
I. Title.

PZ8.7.W5Ho       817'.5'408        74-4044
ISBN 0-8164-3123-X

Jokes travel all over the world and down the centuries. It is hard to discover where they originate. A good example of how a joke travels is the one about a famous court jester in 16th-century France, who stood in front of the mirror with his eyes closed because he wanted to see how he looked when he was asleep. This joke has been told in many different periods, and in many different countries. It is also included in this book, in a slightly altered form.

1570 A.D.

"Is a ton of coal very much, Dad?"

"Well, Son, that depends on whether you're buying it or shoveling it."

"What's the difference between a flea and a camel?" Bob asked Bess.

Bess shook her head.

"A flea can sit on a camel, but a camel can't sit on a flea."

"Why does a young lady depend on the letter Y?"

"Because without it she'd be a lad."

"Mom, is it better to do my homework on an empty stomach or on a full stomach?"

"Better do it on paper, dear."

The house across the street was on fire and Bob rushed to the telephone to call the fire department.

"Hello, hello, is this the fire department?"

"Yes, what is it?"

"Where's the nearest fire box? I want to turn in an alarm!"

11

PETE: I can tell you the score of the baseball game before it starts.

BOB: What is it?

PETE: Nothing to nothing.

TEACHER: Name three collective nouns.

PETE: Flypaper, wastebasket, and vacuum cleaner.

"Well, Peggy," Aunt Clara said, "I hear you went to the dentist. Were you brave?"

"Yes, Auntie. Very."

"Good, here's a quarter. Buy yourself some ice cream. And now tell me what the dentist did."

"He pulled out two of Bob's teeth."

"Yes," said the boastful Charlie, "my family can trace their ancestors back to Columbus."

"Next time," said Pete, "you'll be telling me that your ancestors were in the Ark with Noah."

"Certainly not," Charlie said. "My people had a boat of their own!"

PETE: I bet I can jump across the street.

PEGGY: I bet you can't.

PETE: Watch me cross the street and jump over there!

BETTY: What happened to your thumb?

BOB: I hit the wrong nail!

"I can't let you have the hammer, Bob. You'll hit your thumb again."

"No I won't, Pop. Bess is going to hold the nails."

PEGGY: My girl friend has a twin.

PETE: How can you tell them apart?

PEGGY: Her brother is taller.

After much urging from her mother, Bess wrote the following thank-you note:

"Dear Auntie: Thank you for your nice present. I always wanted a hairbrush, but not very much."

Why does a surgeon wear a mask while performing an operation?

So that after the operation the patient won't know who gave him so much pain.

# A FISH STORY WITH A CATCH

"Poor man, you've lost one of your shoes!"

"No, I haven't. I've just found one."

"What's that book you have?"

"It's called *Happy-Go-Lucky*."

"And the other one?"

"The same, Daddy."

"My teacher said it's very good, so I want to read it twice."

PEGGY: Pete, you're wearing a new shoe style—one red and one black!

PETE: Yes, and what's more, I've got another pair just like it at home.

BETTY: Does your umbrella leak like this all the time?

BOB: Only when it rains.

PEGGY: I wonder what I look like asleep?

PETE: That's easy. Look into the mirror and close your eyes.

"That medicine makes my arm smart."

"Better rub some on your head."

PEGGY: Gracious! Who gave you the black eye, Pete?

PETE: Nobody. I had to fight for it.

"Your picture of the horse isn't bad," Pete said to his little sister Bess. "But where is the wagon?"

"Oh," replied the little artist, "the horse will draw that."

"Why does a donkey like thistles better than corn?"

"Because he's an ass!"

MOTHER AT LUNCH: Your face is clean, but how did you get your hands so dirty?

BOB: Washing my face.

"My horse knows as much as I do."

"Don't tell anybody. You might want to sell him some day."

"Are your father and mother at home?"

"They was in, but they's out now."

"They *was* in, they *is* out? Where is your grammar?"

"She's gone upstairs for a nap."

"Bob, why did you put a mouse in your little sister's bed?" asked Mother.

"Because I couldn't catch a frog."

BOB: I'm so glad they named me Bob.

BESS: Why?

BOB: Because that's what everybody calls me.

"What's the weather like?"

"I don't know. It's so foggy I can't see."

"Can someone name a liquid that doesn't freeze?" asked the teacher.

Bess spoke up: "Warm water, teacher."

MOTHER: Bob, why are you scratching yourself?

BOB: No one else knows where I itch.

MOTHER: Pete, I'm told you went to the ball game instead of going to school.

PETE: That's a lie—and I've got the fish to prove it!

"I've invented something so that people can go through walls," Pete boasted.

"How wonderful!" said Peggy. "What are you going to call it?"

"A door."

Mother was teaching Bess. "Now, dear, what comes after *G*?"

"Whiz!" said Bess.

"Give me a double ice cream sundae with lots of nuts and whipped cream!"

"Would you like a cherry on top?"

"No, thanks. I'm on a diet."

BESS: Yesterday my parents took me out to dinner at a very expensive restaurant.

BOB: What did you have to eat?

BESS: Filet of sole.

BOB: Oh my, that must have been hard to swallow.

PEGGY: You better keep your eyes open tomorrow.

PETE: Why?

PEGGY: You might bump into something if you don't!

What's the difference between a hill and a pill?

A hill is hard to get up and a pill is hard to get down.

"Pete," asked the teacher, "can you tell me where hip-popotamuses are found?"

"Hippopotamuses," answered Pete, "are so big they hardly ever get lost."

Bob took his little sister Bess to a track meet. The one-hundred yard dash had just started.

Bess: Why are they running so fast?

Bob: The first one gets a prize.

Bess: Then why are they *all* running?

PEGGY: Oh, Bob! You've been fighting again and lost a tooth.

BOB: No I didn't, Sis. I've got it in my pocket.

PETE: What has four feet, is gray, and has a trunk?

PEGGY: An elephant, of course.

PETE: Wrong! A gray cat going on vacation.

Little Bob was holding a big stick in his hand.

"What's that stick for?" his mother asked.

"I'm afraid of our neighbor's dog," said Bob. "He always barks at me when I go by."

"Don't be afraid, Son, a barking dog never bites."

"Well, Mom, you know it and I know it—but does the dog know it?"

MOTHER TO GROCER: I sent my little boy to buy two pounds of cherries, and he brought home only a pound and a half.

GROCER: Madam, my scales are all right, but have you weighed your little boy?

PEGGY: When you eat this apple look out for worms, Bobby.

BOB: When I eat an apple the worms better look out for themselves!

"Define a sure-footed man."

"A sure-footed man is a man who, when he kicks, never misses."

At the museum Peggy and Pete saw an Egyptian mummy with the inscription: B. C. 2050.

"What do you make of that number, Pete?"

"I don't know for sure, Peggy. But maybe it's the license number of the car that killed him."

# THE FARMER WHO LAID AN EGG

The class was assembled in the auditorium for the second rehearsal of the school chorus. The music teacher raised his baton, but suddenly stopped and asked in astonishment:

"Bob, why are you standing on a stepladder?"

"Because at yesterday's rehearsal you told me to sing higher."

Pete was having difficulty with his arithmetic homework. In desperation he asked his father, "Won't you do
it for me, Daddy?"

"I'm afraid it wouldn't be right," objected his father.

"But you could at least try," said Pete.

In October the first-graders took a trip to the country.
They watched a flight of migrating birds and the teacher
asked: "Why do birds fly south for the winter?"

No answer.

Suddenly a voice piped up: "Because they can't walk."

"Mommy, I just sold our dog to a friend for one hundred dollars!"

"One hundred dollars! Let me see the money."

"I didn't get any money. I got his two kittens worth fifty dollars each."

"What did you get that little bronze medal for?"

"For playing the trumpet."

"And this nice silver cup?"

"For stopping."

"Today is the twentieth anniversary of an important historical event," said the teacher. "Bob, can you tell me what happened on this special date?"

"I can't remember," said Bob. "I'm only seven years old."

"Naughty boy!" cried Mother. "Why did you hit little Bess?"

"We were playing Adam and Eve, and instead of offering me the apple she ate it herself!"

Father read Pete's report card and frowned.

"English: poor. Mathematics: fair. Science: weak."

"But Dad," said Pete, pointing to the next line, "have you seen this? Health: excellent."

MOTHER: Bob, what happened to you? Your shirt is full of holes!

BOB: Oh, we were playing grocery store and I was the Swiss cheese.

What the Ice said:
"Keep cool."

What the Calendar said:
"Be up-to-date."

What the Fire said:
"Make light of everything."

What the Glue said:
"Find a good thing and stick to it."